BRITAIN IN OLD PHOTOGRAPHS

PETERBOROUGH

LISA SARGOOD

The History Press

CONTENTS

First published in 1996 by Sutton Publishing

This edition first published in 2010 by
The History Press
The Mill, Brimscombe Port,
Stroud, Gloucestershire, GL5 2QG
www.thehistorypress.co.uk

British Library Cataloguing in Publication Data
A catalogue record for this book is available from the
British Library.

ISBN 0-7509-1358-4

Typeset in 10/12 Perpetua.
Typesetting and origination by
Sutton Publishing Limited.
Printed in Great Britain.

Peterborough Museum and Art Gallery

P·M·A·G
Peterborough Museum & Art Gallery

The Museum and Art Gallery covers all aspects of the story of Peterborough, from the distant past to the present day. Displays reveal the prehistoric marine reptiles that lived in the area in the Jurassic period, and the many fascinating everyday items left by our ancestors, from the Romans 2,000 years ago to the medieval monks and much later the Victorians who helped to create the Peterborough we know today. In particular the museum holds a unique collection of bone and wood models made by Napoleonic prisoners of war who were imprisoned at nearby Norman Cross between 1797 and 1814.

The Museum and Art Gallery has a lively programme of temporary exhibitions, including an ever-changing visual arts programme. Our excellent education service provides a wide variety of workshops and handling sessions to reveal the full breadth of the collections to local people.

The museum building itself dates from 1816; it later became the city hospital until it was given to the city as the museum in 1931. Entry is free, disabled access is available to all main floors and the museum has a well-stocked shop.

Admission: Free
Opening times: Tuesday–Saturday, 10 a.m.–5 p.m.
Closed: New Year's Day, Good Friday and Christmas week
Peterborough Museum and Art Gallery · Priestgate · Peterborough PE1 1LF
Tel: 01733 343329 · Fax: 01733 341928

Westgate Congregational Chapel after the fire of 11 January 1891.

Market Square (now Cathedral Square), *c.* 1892: a view of the south side of the Guildhall taken near the site of the old Butter Cross, a small covered market house administered by the Feoffees. After the Restoration of Charles II they gathered donations to build the Chamber over the Cross, or Guildhall as it is now known.

INTRODUCTION

The tale of this city in the Fenland, the story of Peterborough, begins with the founding of the first Saxon monastery here in AD 655 by the Mercian King Paeda. From this early settlement sprang up the town of Medeshamstede, where a peaceful community existed until the destruction wrought by the Danes in AD 870. The Danes' influence on the town is still evident in its street names. The profusion of 'gates' which seems to suggest historical fortifications actually comes from the Danish for 'way'. Hence Cumbergate is the way of the woolcombers, and Westgate the way of the weavers.

The cathedral, which took over a hundred years to complete, is an elegant example of the fusion of Norman and Early English Gothic architecture. It survived the Reformation intact, possibly because Henry VIII's first wife, Catherine of Aragon, is buried within its walls. After a brief period of transition, when the last abbot (later the first bishop) was forced to find alternative employment as schoolmaster in the former monastery, the abbey became one of five new cathedral foundations, gaining its own bishop and diocese in 1541.

The church also weathered the actions of Cromwell's soldiers who ransacked its libraries and destroyed much of its stained glass, including the irreplaceable cloister depictions of Old Testament stories. The stone was sold for profit to Oliver St John and used in the construction of nearby Thorpe Hall. Memorials fared little better. Sir Humphrey Orme, notorious Cavalier and city MP, erected his own memorial tablet in the cathedral years before his death to save his heirs the expense and so lived to witness its destruction.

Yet this book is not just a history of the cathedral, for the town which grew up around its walls, its shops and markets, fairs and everyday street-life are just as fascinating and tell much about the ability of Peterborough's citizens to adapt to changing rural practices, the advent of new forms of transport and ways of working. Until the late eighteenth century the population of Peterborough remained fairly consistent but the Industrial Revolution and the coming of the railways were to alter its character considerably. Its traditional fairs grew in size and became more of a public entertainment while its markets attracted new trades and its streets threw up ever increasing numbers of hotels and public houses to accommodate visitors. A new iron bridge replaced the ancient wooden one and the streets became criss-crossed with tramlines. At the end of the nineteenth century the population had grown to about 28,000 and new housing was emerging from the ruins of Peterborough's past: the stone from Boroughbury Tithe Barn was sold, and went towards building Rothesay Villas in 1892. But it was probably the demolition of Narrow Bridge Street to lay foundations for the Town Hall that heralded the advent of the city's development into the place Peterborough now appears. In 1964 a government study of the south-east recommended Peterborough for New Town status. So began the transformation of a medium-sized market town encircled by engineering factories into the modern city centre it is today.

This photographic journey through the city's past begins in the reign of Queen Victoria and closes in that of her great-grandson George VI. It documents a place slowly absorbing the industrial innovations of the last two centuries, and many of the views presented here no longer exist. The Queensgate development incorporated some the city's finest old buildings but levelled many others. These pictures show how the city developed schools, emergency services, fighting forces and institutions to help the poor, founded museums and built libraries, spotlighting a few characters who made particular contributions in the process. Yet throughout these changes the cathedral, Guildhall and River Nene, silent witnesses to the city's work, sport and celebration remain unchanged, and enough clues to the past exist for new and old Peterborians alike to trace the heritage of their home town.

The Market Square was decorated for the visit of Prince George on 28 June 1929.

CHAPTER ONE

THE CATHEDRAL & PRECINCTS

Cathedral, west front detail, c. 1886. An old local rhyme tells that 'Peterborough Minster would not have been so high, If Barnack Quarry had not been so nigh'. The grandeur and beauty of the Cathedral Church of St Peter, St Paul and St Andrew is indisputable. The west front has been called 'the most magnificent portico in Christendom'.

Cathedral, west front, *c.* 1886. The fine triple arches of the west front are seen from the chancel of St Thomas the Martyr's chapel. Completed early in the fourteenth century, the façade reveals the subtle change in character as the new Gothic style crept into the original Norman design, begun with the east end of the building in 1118. The central porch beneath the Trinity chapel was constructed in the early fourteenth century in Perpendicular style. To the left lies the gate to the monks' cemetery on the cathedral's north side. Adjacent stands the Deanery Gate, built in about 1500, entrance to the Prior's Lodging and supposedly the way into Abbot Kirkton's Deer Park.

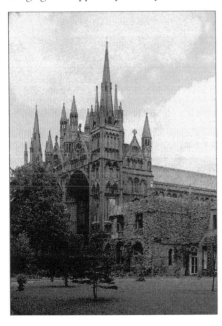

A view of the west front from the south-west, *c.* 1886. This is the third church on the site. The first Saxon monastery was built in about AD 655 by King Paeda of Mercia and survived until desecrated by the Danes in about AD 870. A century later a Benedictine order adopted the site, building a church that was destroyed by fire in 1116. In 1118 the present Norman church was begun, taking over a hundred years to complete. It survived the Reformation and in 1541 became one of five new cathedral foundations. It has been the resting-place of Queen Catherine of Aragon, unfortunate consort of Henry VIII, who died at nearby Kimbolton, and Mary, Queen of Scots, beheaded at Fotheringay Castle and buried by the gravedigger Old Scarlett on 1 August 1587. Mary's body was later removed to Westminster Abbey by order of her son, King James I.

The upper part of the eastern end, 'New Building', from the rear of the precincts, late 1860s. This was constructed by Abbot Kirkton in about 1510. The beauty of the fan-vaulted interior is reminiscent of that at King's College Chapel, Cambridge, and is probably by the same mason, John Wastell.

Cathedral, north side, *c.* 1882. In 1883 J.L. Pearson set about the task of rebuilding the north side of the cathedral, which had been found to be subsiding twenty years earlier during work on the wooden roof of the apse. A local builder, John Thompson, was contracted to remove the tower, improve its foundations and rebuild it. This work required numbering each stone as the tower was deconstructed and took six years to complete. During this operation a decision was taken to remove 'Kipling's Chimneys' (named after Dean Kipling), which are still evident in this 1882 photograph.

Monastic Infirmary Arches, *c.* 1882. These elegant and now fragile arches are part of the remains of the original monks' hospital, built by Abbot John de Caux between 1250 and 1262.

Cathedral, Canon's or Bishop's Door, *c.* 1886. A classic example of Norman architectural design. The boys with their caps are probably from King's School in the cathedral precincts. Opposite this door are the remains of the cloisters and monks' lavatorium which were desecrated by Cromwellians in about 1650. Within the cloisters a hastily dug graveyard has been unearthed which may contain the bones of monks massacred by the Danes in *c.* AD 870. Miss Gibson's School, Laurel Court, where Edith Cavell was pupil-teacher, over-looked the site for fifty years.

Galilee Court, *c.* 1886. This view, taken from the west front, shows St Nicholas' Gateway, built by Abbot Benedict in the twelfth century, with the Guildhall behind and the tower of St John's church beyond. On the right is the chancel of St Thomas the Martyr's chapel, where a casket holding the saint's relics was displayed. It was the city's first museum, and with the adjacent building formed part of King's School. To the left lies the Bishop's gateway and Knights' Chamber, dating from the time when the abbot had to keep an army of knights for service to the king.

The Bishop's Palace, *c.* 1896. Within the cathedral precincts laypeople lived and worked, supporting the bishop and his retinue. This gathering may be the staff of the bishop's residence, which employed a cook, gardener and maids, a much reduced number from the days when bishops held almost regal status and were expected to entertain princes at their table. Prince Henry, later Henry VIII, dined regularly with the abbot in Peterborough when the latter was JP of the city.

Cathedral bell tower, 1886. This striking and unusual picture of the city taken from the bell tower provides a close-up of the intricate stonework of its pinnacles. Peterborough's four bells were cast in the city at Henry Penn's foundry in Bridge Street in 1709.

SECTION TWO

CITY STREETS

Boroughbury Manor House, c. 1920. Sadly demolished in January 1915, Boroughbury Manor was home to many of Peterborough's notables including Thomas Deacon MP, founder of Deacon's School, and the Cavalier Sir Humphrey Orme MP. Originally part of the Abbey Farm, it was built as the abbot's residence by Godfrey of Crowland in 1307. He was also responsible for the Bishop's Gateway and Knight's Chamber in Galilee Court at the cathedral.

Boroughbury Barn, *c.* 1890. This was the smaller of two Boroughbury barns built in the twelfth century by Abbot Adam Boothby as part of the Abbey's Manor Farm. This farm with its large fish-ponds rendered the community virtually self-sufficient for centuries. The barns were used to store wheat and barley and were constructed of stone, chestnut and oak. One was demolished at the time of the Civil War, but this one survived until 1890 when it was bought by James McCallum Craig. He removed the stone, selling it to the builders of nearby Rothesay Villas in 1892.

The interior of Boroughbury Barn before demolition, *c.* 1890. Also known as the Tithe Barn, it was one of several medieval tithe barns in Peterborough; these included the Sexton Barns at the Sacristan's Farm (once near the railway station site).

Boroughbury Maltings, 1898. Note the distinctive chimney of the maltings and the old-fashioned uniform worn by the soldier, from the Volunteer Rifle Corps. This was later the site of the city's Liberal Party HQ and it was here that George Greenwood gave his triumphant speech after the 1906 election. After he had moved to an hotel, his supporters set light to his carriage and dragged the burning coach to the Conservative Party's HQ at the Angel in Narrow Bridge Street.

Thorpe Park Lodge, c. 1910. The Park Lodge stood by the gateway on the road to Thorpe Hall. The Hall was built between 1653 and 1656 by Oliver St John using material from the ruins of the cathedral lady chapel. It has been home to the Fitzwilliam and Strong families. It was leased by the Peterborough District Hospital Board in 1939 and is now a Sue Ryder hospice.

Market Place, *c.* 1910. The pitched cover for the market stalls belonged to Peach & Sons of Peterborough and J. Toogood, strawberry grower at Alwalton. The women's fashions show the latent influence of the sombre Victorian contrasting with the jaunty Edwardian boaters worn here.

Market Square, *c.* 1914. The exact date of this picture is uncertain but may be guessed from what appear to be recruiting posters for the Royal Navy tied to the Guildhall railings. The building immediately behind the Guildhall was a temporary police station in the 1950s, now demolished. Horse-drawn cabs could be hired from the ranks by St John's church and regularly carried men out to Hicks brickworks at Fletton. The tram network was unable to reach that side of town because of the impediment of Narrow Street, and because the Great Eastern Railway would not allow their line to be crossed at London Road.

Market-place and Guildhall, *c.* 1905. The present Guildhall was built by the Feoffees in 1671 with public subscriptions, Earl Fitzwilliam offering £20 if the arms of King Charles II were incorporated into John Lovin's Dutch-style design. It occupies the site of the Butter Cross, a covered area used by women selling butter and cheese, near the original Guildhall and Moot Hall. It has fulfilled many functions, being the Town Hall between 1874 and 1933. To the left of the picture is the Gates Memorial (absent from the picture below), unveiled in 1897.

Market-place and Guildhall, *c.* 1897. Peterborough was granted a charter to hold markets on Wednesday and Saturday by King Edgar in about AD 980. Market Square became the city's trading centre when the 'Marketstede' was relocated west of the Cathedral by Abbot Martin in 1200. Market tribunals and public whippings were carried out here and the city's stocks were located north of the Guildhall. The elegant town houses to the right of the Guildhall formed part of the Town Hall until their demolition in March 1923.

Market Place and St Nicholas's Gateway, *c.* 1905. From 1903 trams were stopping at the market-place, bringing increasing numbers of people to the city. To the far left of the picture is Wrigley's Clothiers, later to become the offices of the Canadian emigration service. Next is the site of the future Lloyds Bank while on the other side of the gate is Caster's printing works. Adjacent is the depot of the London Clothing Company, previously Simpson & White's Bank.

Market Place, *c.* 1890. The market-place was originally known as the Marketstede and later Market Square. In the early 1960s when the city council moved the market to the cattle market site off Broadway it was renamed Cathedral Square.

St Nicholas's Gateway, *c.* 1913. Burlingham's shop by the Gateway was demolished in 1913 to make way for a new bank. The Becket casket, containing relics of the saint (brought to Peterborough by Abbot Benedict in 1180), was auctioned by Sotheby's in 1981 and is now in the Victoria Albert Museum. The clock faces on the lamppost to the left were the tram timetables and mark the terminus for Eastfield, Walton and Thorpe. The Cathedral Studio and Art Gallery was situated to the right of the Gateway, opposite the former offices of coal merchants J. Fairweather and Sons.

Market Place, early 1920s. Caster and Jelley's print works are shown here boarded up prior to demolition, the window displaying a 'relocated to Cowgate' poster. J.W. Williamson's toyshop, previously Foot's hat warehouse, offers a 'rebuilding sale'. The fine eighteenth-century building of the removal company London Furnishings disappeared when the east side of Narrow Street was demolished to make way for the new Town Hall.

Narrow Bridge Street, 21 October 1929. So called because it was just 20 ft from pavement to pavement, Narrow Bridge Street underwent a transformation in 1929, becoming part of Broad Bridge Street when its eastern side was demolished. The road was known thereafter as Bridge Street and it was here that the Town Hall foundation stone was laid by Prince George. To the left of the top picture is an advert for the City cinema in Bridge Street, one of Peterborough's three picture-houses at the time. In the bottom picture it is possible to make out the distinctive 'B' of the Boots the Chemist's logo. The first Boots branch opened in Narrow Bridge Street in1894 with a second opening in Westgate in 1902. In 1911 the company built its largest shop in the market-place; its ornate black and white plasterwork interspersed with colourful effigies can still be seen.

Narrow Bridge Street, *c.* 1920. Peterborough's most controversial building when it was proposed, the Midland Bank still occupies this site on the corner of Cathedral Square and Bridge Street. In 1895 the National Telephone Company set up its offices in Pearson's at this end of the street. Paviour's clock seen on the left was built by Mr Whatley Paviour who ran a watchmaker's shop here. The skeleton design is very unusual as the mechanism is situated at a distance from the face and hands. It kept 'railway time', an advantage to the townspeople as the church clocks were notoriously unreliable. When Mr Whatley Paviour retired in 1902 he sold the shop to Messrs Barron Clark and left the clock to the city. Its face now graces the front of the old library in Broadway but its mechanism is in the Priestgate Museum.

Narrow Bridge Street, 1915: a view from the corner of Broad Bridge Street. On the left of the street is the parcels and reservations office of the Great Northern Railway. The number of soldiers in differing uniforms walking past this office is a reminder of the number of troops billeted in and around the city during the First World War.

Narrow Bridge Street, 1916 or later. On the left beyond the Grand Hotel's sign is the sign of the Angel. This hotel and hostelry existed for over 500 years until demolished in 1972. It was an important venue for travelling players, weddings and public occasions and was also the site of the city's cock-fighting pit. By tradition it was the headquarters of the local Conservative Association and on election day it was common for townspeople to try to roll a burning barrel up the front steps – a practice discouraged by one landlord who armed his guests with pans of water to throw over the revellers. On the left notice the first F.W. Woolworth store in the city opposite Murkett's garage, which took over the Golden Lion Hotel.

Narrow Bridge Street, *c.* 1890. This fragment of the street provides a wealth of detail. Gazing at the photographer is Mr Richard Andrew ('Authorised Plumber') and on the right of his arched doorway the stationery and photography business run by the Martin family. To the left is the florist's window of W.& J. Brown; the garlands suggest that it may be springtime, as these were traditional in Peterborough in May.

Waggon & Horses, Bridge Street, *c.* 1920. Seen here next to F.W. Woolworth, the Waggon & Horses pub yard was the venue during the latter half of the last century of the Skin Market. The sheepskin and hide sellers transferred here from a site in Cumbergate. It was also the first home of the Peterborough Agricultural Society's annual show.

Spread Eagle, Broad Bridge Street, *c.* 1923. Next to one of Neaverson's famous tea-rooms, this public house was one of the city's carrier stations. Several of these early haulage contractors stabled their horses in its yard on Wednesday and Saturday in anticipation of market business. They provided a valuable service to outlying villages, bringing in fresh produce and returning from the city with orders.

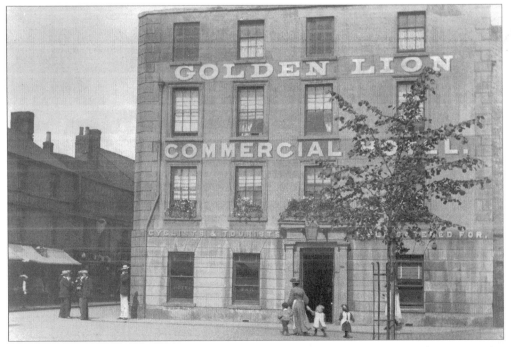

Commercial Hotel, Bridge Street, *c.* 1905. The Golden Lion marked the junction of Narrow Bridge Street and Broad Bridge Street. It was to become Murkett's garage before its demolition with the rest of the east side of Narrow Street in 1928.

Broad Bridge Street, before 1901. Wells's coopers workshop advertises 'shavings for smoking hams' and a soon to be performed opera. An interesting detail is the plaque above the name sign which reads 'Fireman'. To speed up fire service attendance the National Telephone Company installed call-bells at the home of each of the city's firemen in 1902. This enamel plate helped townspeople to raise the alarm more quickly.

Broad Bridge Street, looking south to the Town Bridge, before 1901. Jauncey's ironmongers, cutlery grinder and machine repair shop, seen on an unusually quiet day. Ironmongery became one of the city's most important services after the advent of agricultural machinery in the nineteenth century.

Broad Bridge Street, 1890s. The Saracens Head Hotel and public house was run by the Dell family at the time this picture was taken. Outside stands the carrier's cart. It was also the departure point of the 'Peterborough Diligence', which travelled to Holborn from Peterborough during the eighteenth and nineteenth centuries.

E. Jarvis & Sons, harness maker's shop, Long Causeway, c. 1890. This beautiful photograph of a traditional leather-worker's business shows the jars and bottles in the windows containing horse liniment and leather polishes.

Broad Bridge Street, 1920s: a view of the River Nene from the south bank with the iron Town Bridge, opened in 1872, on the left. Opposite, just out of view, is the eighteenth-century Customs House and the mooring platform used by barges and pleasure craft. It was here that travelling players would perform and ferries depart for Wisbech. The Temperance Hotel stands sentry at the bridge.

New Bridge, *c.* 1934. The city's first bridge across the Nene was wooden and built by Abbot Martin in 1308. Its maintenance was in constant dispute as he neglected to make provision for its upkeep and indeed the first structure was so flimsy that it was swept away. The second bridge, built with two stone supports, lasted until 1872, when it was replaced with an iron one, paid for by public subscription. J.L. Speight & Co. Ltd completed the present concrete bridge, twice the width of its predecessors, in 1934.

Hunting Orland & Co.'s tobacco shop in Narrow Street. This elegant shop-front with its late-Victorian/early-Edwardian lamps and colourful display must have been a spectacle. Many of the brands here displayed, Players and Woodbine, for example, are still in existence.

Park Road, between 1889 and 1896. The sheep are being driven along Park Road past the Co-operative Society's store. This large and impressive shop sold a range of local goods and included a tailor, shoe-shop and grocery.

Long Causeway, *c.* 1911. T.L. Barrett's store is shown here decorated for the coronation of King George V. Mr T.L. Barrett was mayor of Peterborough twice, in 1888 and 1889, and died in September 1919.

The basket-weaver's stall, Long Causeway, *c.* 1900. The city was granted the right to hold a market in Cathedral Square in AD 972 but the traders overflowed into the city's streets on market day. These baskets were probably made by Mr Hubbard, who had work premises in Cumbergate as well as a shop in Westgate. The cane for weaving was collected from willow growing between Woodston and Orton and peeled by hand by local women.

Bull Hotel, Westgate, *c.* 1890. The Bull Hotel was one of Peterborough's best hotels, competing with the Royal nearby, the Angel in Bridge Street and the Talbot in Market Place. It is thought to date from the seventeenth century and its front is little changed apart from the addition in about 1900 of an extra storey. In the background are the twin spires of the Congregational church burnt down in 1891. The cart on the left belonged to 'Toffee King' J. Richer.

Westgate, *c.* 1890. This view of Westgate is from the opposite end of the street, near the Malt & Shovel pub with the Congregational church on the left. The man walking towards the photographer on the left appears to be a railway worker.

Mansion House, Westgate, *c.* 1911. The Mansion House dominated the corner of Westgate near the Bull Hotel. It was the home of famous city campanologist Matthew Wyldbore (1722–87), Peterborough's MP in 1768. His legacy to pay for the bells of St John's to be rung on 15 March every year was an expression of his thanks to the church, whose bells guided him to safety when he became lost in the Fens one misty night. This imposing house was also the home of Dr Leonard Cane and other city physicians until it was demolished in about 1925.

Wortley's Almshouses, Westgate, *c.* 1910. This site was purchased by city MP Edward Wortley in 1744. Local legend tells that Dickens paid a visit here in about 1836 while writing *Oliver Twist*: not much of a recommendation! In 1837 the Board of Guardians established a new workhouse for Peterborough Union in Thorpe Road and the Feoffees converted this building into Tudor-style almshouses. The building is now a pub, but the Wortley plaque remains above the door.

'The Largest Chemists in the World': another Boots' shop in the city, Westgate, *c.* 1905. Their early confidence seems to have been justified. The Nottingham company's empire now stretches far beyond Peterborough's streets.

Deacon Street lokking towards Queen Street, October 1905. Hutchinson's Depot was situated in Queen's Street and cabs like the one on the left could be hired from them. The other vehicle is agricultural and was probably made by Barford and Perkins, agricultural engineers based in the city and most famous for their rollers.

Queen Street, *c.* 1915. T. Hill & Sons Maltings established premises here in 1854 and operated a wharf on the river between the Town Bridge and the viaduct to bring malt into the city. Malt for brewing had been an important commodity in Peterborough since before the Restoration as the water supplies were notoriously filthy and most of the populace preferred the taste of ale!

Westgate, *c.* 1900. The Black Horse near Boroughbury corner at the junction of Westgate and Lincoln Road provides a rare example of regional architecture with its low sloping dormer windows. The adjacent square building has changed use many times. Here it is the premises of the local undertaker C. Thompson, but it had previously been a milliner's shop.

Cowgate, c. 1905. The city's first graveyard was situated at the far end of Cowgate and was the hunting-ground of Peterborough's very own Burke and Hare. In 1828 a series of grave-robbings were carried out and a body discovered in the nearby garden of a city doctor. This end of the street was also the site of the first public dispensary, opened in May 1816 with Dr Skrimshire as physician. This scene changed when the building of Crescent Bridge commenced in 1911.

The Commercial Hotel near the station, Cowgate, 28 October 1911. Note the sign on the left advising 'Beware of Pickpockets'. The number of hotels and public houses in Peterborough burgeoned with the advent of the railway; during the latter half of the last century the city had more than sixty hostelries.

Church Street, *c.* 1940. Next to the imposing shop-front of C.A. Barlow's shop near the Corn Exchange is one of the city's ARP shelters. Adjacent is the ARP stores and station of the Wardens & Fire Guard.

Church Street, 1897. The false portcullis through which the Hutchinson's Draper's cart is passing is part of the street decoration for Queen Victoria's diamond jubilee. Such events had tremendous significance for the city population: for many it was a public holiday, while for others such as workhouse-dwellers and for schoolchildren special teas were arranged by city officials.

Cowgate, *c.* 1900. Deacon's school was established in Cowgate in 1721 under the terms of the will of Thomas Deacon, MP and public benefactor, whose ornate memorial can be seen in the 'New Building' of the cathedral. It was founded for the education of boys, but merged with Mrs Ireland's school (housed in the Guildhall for sixty years) in 1874. At the new school in Deacon Street the city's first telephone was answered on 9 February 1878.

St Leonard's Street, Fitzwilliam Cottages, *c.* 1895. The street probably took its name from the leper hospital situated near Spital Bridge, whose chapel was dedicated to St Leonard, patron saint of the sick. The area was known by most of the population, however, as the 'Common Muckhill'! As late as 1861 it housed a sedan chair business and in 1867 the 1st Northants Engineers (Redcoats), founded by Leonard Deacon, built their headquarters here.

St Leonard's Street, *c.* 1895. This wooden building at the junction with Milton Street has a fascinating history. It was constructed from timbers bought at auction in 1816 when the Norman Cross POW barracks were demolished. At the end of the Napoleonic Wars the last of the 10,000 French prisoners and the British regiments that policed them left Peterborough, dramatically affecting the city's economy.

Cumbergate, *c.* 1890. Cumbergate, the street of the medieval woolcombers, is now partly submerged beneath the Queensgate centre. Duddington's ironmongers operated here before moving to the opposite corner (left), having had the premises completely rebuilt. They later opened a second shop in Westgate. The sign on the right reads 'To the Post Office', this being the large building in the middle of the row. In 1833 the city's first post office opened in Priestgate on the corner of Wentworth Street. Mr James Gates became its first postmaster. Increasing demand for postal services necessitated moves to the market-place and Long Causeway before transferring to this purpose-built site in Cumbergate in 1874.

The turn of the alleyway by the side of the post office which led to Brainsby's carriage works, Cumbergate, *c.* 1890. This was the site of a disastrous fire in 1898. On the corner is an unusual seventeenth-century building, which was occupied by the saddler E.A. Law until its demolition, when the post office expanded and built a new sorting office on the site.

A view of Cumbergate where it meets Exchange Street with St John's church at the end, 1903. On the left are the old East Almshouses, which were demolished in 1904 to be replaced by those built with a legacy of £5,000 from Miss Pears. Mr James Harrison 'Postcard' Smith came to live here following his retirement in 1940. The postcards referred to were those he sold at his shop in Cumbergate. The street also housed the Feofees Bridewell House of Correction, the city's first public gaol, demolished in 1844.

Cumbergate and St John's church, *c.* 1902. To the right of the picture are the White Horse Inn and Coach & Horses pub. Dominating the scene is the tower of St John's church, built here when the parish church was resited west of the cathedral from its previous home in Boongate.

Exchange Street, looking east towards the cathedral, *c.* 1890. Halfway down is the junction with Cumbergate leading to the post office. The headquarters of the Peterborough City Fire Brigade was on the corner of Cumbergate in 1872, and moved to Wood Street before moving to Deacon Street in about 1900. At the far end of the street is the Talbot Hotel with its distinctive bay windows. Now demolished, it was the Boston and Hull coaching stop. On the left of the picture is P.J. Whyman's umbrella repair shop next to the Hair-cutting room.

Cumbergate, *c.* 1903. This shows the demolition of the garden wall of the old almshouses built by the Feoffees. The new almshouses (in the background) were occupied at the beginning of 1904. The Moot Hall, also administered by the Feoffees, was originally sited here until its demolition in about 1610.

Miss Pears's Almhouses, on the corner of Cumbergate, 1930s. Miss Pears was the daughter of a city draper and died in 1901. Her legacy of £5,000 was then a considerable sum. The almshouses are now a restaurant. When the Queensgate development was proposed a number of buildings here were incorporated into the design, having been 'listed' by the Department of the Environment.

Priestgate, above and right, *c.* 1894. Its name meaning simply 'way of the Priests', the origins of this street are now obscure. Priestgate has long been one of the city's more select residential areas. The city's first tennis, bowls and squash clubs were here. In the seventeenth and eighteenth centuries the gardens of homes on the south side sloped down to the river, and it was here that Squire Thomas Cooke had his estate and built his prestigious house, now the city's museum. Dominating the view above is the spire of 32 Priestgate, Squire Cooke's Dower House, at the corner of Trinity Street. It was redesigned in 1861 to become the entrance hall of the Trinity Congregational church, which was built in gardens at the rear. In the 1940s it merged with the Presbyterian church and in 1972 moved to St Andrew's in Ledbury Road. The church in Trinity Street was then demolished. The building in the picture on the right was once a vicarage belonging to St John's Church.

This view shows the back streets and ordinary housing of Peterborough's inhabitants, early 1920s. This photograph was taken at the beginning of the Depression which was to hit Peterborough very hard.

St John's Street, Boongate, *c.* 1900. St John's Street and its junction with Eastgate, in the background, marks the original site of Peterborough's market-place and focus of the medieval town. The thatched cottages burnt down on 28 April 1942. Owing to its low-lying position the area was prone to flooding and these streets were often thick with mud. The public preferred to attend services at St Thomas the Martyr's chapel rather than brave this route to their parish church, much to the consternation of the monks.

St John's Vicarage, Boongate, *c.* 1920. The first parish church in Peterborough, St John's was originally sited at Boongate to the east of the cathedral. It was built in the ninth century, but local flooding and the relocation of the city centre by Abbot Genge caused the church to be moved to its present site at Cathedral Square in 1407. The original Boongate vicarage was sold and by the time this picture was taken had been converted to a public house run by W. Shaw, purveyor of 'good beer'. It is known locally as The Marquis of Granby.

John Bull's House, City Road (Howgate), *c.* 1910. John Bull was a local photographer.

Midgate, *c.* 1880: a fragile print of the seventeenth-century façade of the Swan Inn with its distinctive leaded porch and sundial. Note the reassuring notice promising 'well-aired beds' and the advertisement for Stimson's cabs. A later licensee, William Bailey, also ran a highly successful fleet of horse-drawn omnibuses until 1904 when the trams took his trade.

Globe Street, *c.* 1900. This street was situated off Albert Place, now Bourges Boulevard. The Globe pub on a Sunday afternoon was evidently a popular place. The licensee at the time this picture was taken was Frank Peaks.

Midgate, before 1905. Stott's newspaper shop reaches into the street with its billboards for the *Daily Telegraph* and the *Comet*. Peterborough had its own newspapers, with the *Advertiser* founded in 1854 by J.S. Clarke (sold in 1897 to Sir Richard Winfrey who started the East Midlands Allied Press), and the *Standard*, in circulation since 1872. Stott's moved to Westgate in 1905 and the building shown here was demolished in 1906

Westgate, *c.* 1900. Miss Willoughby's school was one of several private girls' boarding schools in the city. Miss Willoughby taught the usual accomplishments: painting, singing and dancing as well as French, German and English. The building had previously been named Westgate House, and had been owned by the Tomlin family.

St John's Middle Class School, Broad Bridge Street, before 1900. After the closure of Mrs Ireland's free school in 1839, which had been held in 'the Chamber over the Cross' (rooms in the Guildhall) since 1800, the boys were sent to Deacon's School and the girls to St John's Middle Class School in Broad Bridge Street. Private education had been available to selected Peterborough students for centuries but it was not until 1824 that the city's first National School opened in Providential Place, off Nelson Street, funded by the Anglican Church. This was followed by the Congregationalists' school in Wood Street in 1852.

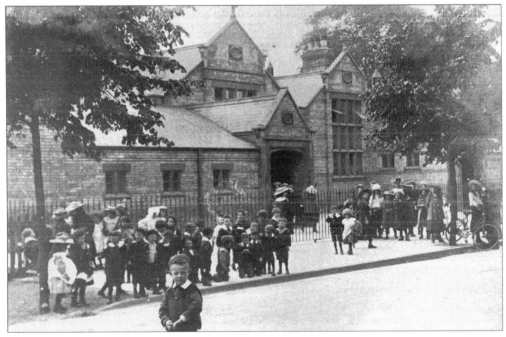

An enchanting photograph of Bishop's Road School, *c.* 1906. The photographer attracted the close attention of one inquisitive schoolboy.

EVENTS &
ENTERTAINMENTS

Lincoln Road, 1902. The Fletton Fire Service parade the streets of Peterborough as part of the city's celebrations for the coronation of Edward VII in 1902.

Cromwell Road, *c.* 1910. A street entertainer makes a meagre living playing the accordion while his monkey dances for a group of children. The boy with the basket may be an errand boy, but is probably collecting money while his partner provokes the miserable monkey with his stick.

Cowgate, on the corner of St Leonard's Street, 1911. Travelling menageries and circus animals were always a great spectacle as they entered the city streets. Zoos were uncommon and wildlife documentaries unknown so the sight of a live elephant always drew large crowds of interested children. Camels, prancing horses and 'Red Indians' also graced the streets to advertise their shows.

The children of Peterborough – most wearing hats – pack the Market Square to commemorate the diamond jubilee of Queen Victoria in 1897. The celebrations commenced on the Sunday before Jubilee Day, hence all the Sunday School banners on display; this also shows the number of Nonconformist churches in the city at the time. They include the Harris Street School, Baptists, Methodists and St Mary's School. Sunday Schools were begun in the city by Bishop Hinchcliffe in about 1769 to promote literacy. At the time only King's and Deacon's schools were in existence. After this rally 6,000 children and their teachers were treated to tea at the Corn Exchange by the City Council.

Westgate, 1897. Plow the florist and other Westgate shopkeepers bedecked their shops for the city's commemoration of Queen Victoria's diamond jubilee.

Long Causeway, looking towards Midgate, 1897. Thomas Stone's office is just visible behind the street's decoration to celebrate the queen's jubilee. To the left of the picture is the delivery van of one of the city's many chemists. Until the late nineteenth century medicine was too expensive for most of the population and many relied on the travelling 'mountebank' or quack doctor selling patent remedies in the streets.

Westgate, *c.* 1912. The rather theatrically dressed woman in these pictures has playing cards pinned to her skirt. The man walking towards her in the top photo is a photographer carrying his camera and tripod. The occasion is a city parade in aid of the Hospital Saturday Fund (started in 1875). This event maintained the hospital before the days of government funding. One hopes her engaging smile proved persuasive to the smart Edwardian gentlemen she has approached in Church Street (below). The colourful poster behind her in the top picture advertises a local production of the *Forty Thieves* while the concert is being held at the Drill Hall. Other principal venues at that time were the Fitzwilliam Room of the Angel Hotel, the Corn Exchange and Wentworth Assembly Room.

Narrow Bridge Street, 1902. The banner on the shop to the left reads 'God Save The King' and the flags are out in celebration of the coronation of Edward VII, belatedly held on 8 August 1902. On this day the City Council provided tea for 600 of Peterborough's poor in the Midland Railway sheds at Thorpe Road and a 'Grand Procession' of over 100 carriages and floats paraded the streets to raise money for a new wing at the Priestgate Infirmary.

Narrow Bridge Street, 1902. A view of the same scene from further along the street showing the façade of the Angel Hotel, demolished in 1972, opposite the shoe store belonging to Freeman, Hardy & Willis. Note the contrast in the clothes worn: the ordinary working man in a brown suit and flat cap, with a pocket watch on a chain, set against the smart black suit, bowler and cane of the city gent.

The Guildhall resplendent for the coronation of Edward VII, Market Square, 1902. On the left corner is the angled façade of the Peterborough branch of the Stamford, Spalding and Boston Banking Company. When this became bankrupt the site was taken over by Barclays, whose original offices were on the opposite side of Market Square. Along the street is the pitched roof of the mobile canteen used by the city's cab drivers.

Cromwell Road, 1902. At the junction with Russell Street is the Steam Engine Inn, later frequented by soldiers billeted in nearby streets during the First World War. Here it is decorated for the coronation of Edward VII. Women's fashions are evidently changing, the length of a respectable hem-line beginning to rise.

Westwood Street, near the corner of Bright Street, 6 June 1896. The City Corporation fire engine parades past Bright Street, followed by a lifeboat, the *Mary Staniford*, from the Sussex coast, to raise money for the Second Annual Lifeboat Day.

Market Square, 14 June 1898. The Gates Memorial was built to honour Peterborough's first mayor, Henry Pearson Gates (1818–93). He presided over the city's conversion to a municipality and at the first council meeting on 28 May 1874 was unanimously elected mayor. The fountain was taken down in 1963 and re-erected in Bishop's Road Gardens in 1967. Note the elegant fashions worn by the women of the time, illustrating the high regard in which Mr Gates was held.

Broadway, *c.* 1913 (above) and *c.* 1950 (below). The Hippodrome opened as Peterborough's second and largest theatre on 17 September 1907. In 1908 it was bought by the music-hall impresario Fred Karno, whose company included Charlie Chaplin, Max Miller and Marie Lloyd. After many successful years its lease passed to Messrs Bancroft, who bought it in 1930. Shortly afterwards the building was demolished. In 1938 local boy Vernon Watson played there with his son as the comedy duo Nosmo King & Hubert, returning again in 1947 in *For the Fun of It* with Frankie Howerd. Opposite is the Kinema or Broadway Electric Theatre Cinematograph, opened in 1911. Just past the Embassy is Cattle Market Road. The livestock market moved there from Long Causeway in 1866.

Memorial Hospital Carnival, *c.* 1929. Looking like something out of *Alice in Wonderland*, this carnival float was raising money for the Midland Road Hospital. The War Memorial Hospital was opened in June 1928 by Field Marshal Sir William Robertson as a lasting reminder of the city's soldiers killed during the First World War.

As part of the celebrations for Edward VII's coronation in 1902 floats paraded the city streets displaying scenes from Peterborough's history. This picture, taken in Westgate at the junction with Cromwell Road, captures the re-enactment of Mary, Queen of Scots going to her execution at Fotherinhay Castle. Towler's in the background appears to be hedging its bets – operating both as a gas fitter and electrical engineer.

Memorial Hospital Carnival, *c.* 1929. No history of Peterborough is complete without mention of Edith Louisa Cavell, heroine of the First World War and resident in Peterborough while pupil-teacher at Miss Gibson's school at Laurel Court. She left the city in 1886 to work as a governess but later trained as a nurse. In 1907 she was offered the post of matron in a Brussels hospital and after the outbreak of the First World War joined the Resistance movement. Hundreds of Allied soldiers smuggled through the hospital owed her their lives. She was arrested in August 1915, court-martialled and shot on 15 October. A plaque in the cathedral commemorates her association with Peterborough.

Regatta Day, *c.* 1914. The Regatta was one of Peterborough's chief social events, held on August Bank Holiday and attracting craft from all over the region. The city's watchmaker, Mr Whatley Paviour, was captain of the Peterborough Rowing Club (founded in about 1875) and Regatta Commander before the event ceased in 1914. This was the last event until the Rowing Club was re-established in 1948.

Skaters on the Nene with the Custom House on the right and the Town Bridge in the background, *c.* 1890. Peterborough's most famous skater was J.W. Rowe, also a champion cyclist and city councillor. Among many triumphs he won the International Amateur Championship at Lingay Fen in 1890.

River Nene, *c.* 1890. Taken from the quay near the Custom House, this scene is reminiscent of Dickens's descriptions of London ice-fairs. Speed-skating races were hosted here to raise funds for Russian refugees during the First World War. The fen-lighters stuck fast in the ice and the English Brothers' building on the right are reminders that this is a working river.

Westgate, *c.* 1900. Girls skipping in the street are dressed in the white smocks designed to keep their black wool dresses clean. As they all wear hats they may be turned out for school. Such charming scenes were lost with the advent of cars and trams.

Bridge Street, *c.* 1900. The girls dressed in white may be celebrating May Day. An old Peterborough custom was to dress orphaned girls in white on this day to parade the streets singing for alms. Other Mayday traditions include the plaiting of the May Garland, a practice revived by Mr John House in 1877 when he hosted a competition in Wellington Lane, displaying the eighty entries in his garden.

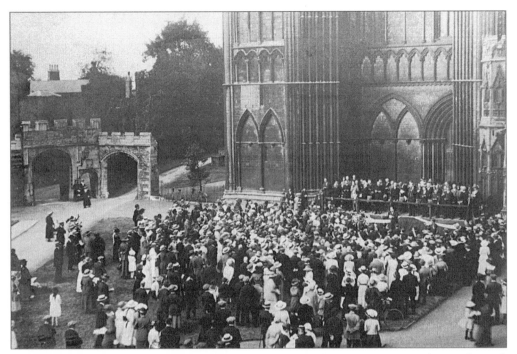

A meeting held on behalf of the League of Nations, Cathedral Close, 25 June 1921. The Peterborough branch was very active; J.W. Bodger, Hon. Curator at Peterborough Museum, was one of its notable members.

Broadway, 28 June 1929. Flag-waving children line part of Prince George's route around the city near the Theatre Royal & Empire. The theatre, originally a public hall, was built by Pye & Hayward for W.D. Nicholls, a city wine merchant, in the 1870s. Its first entrance was in Park Road. In 1894 it became the Theatre Royal and was temporarily renamed The Grand in 1916. It closed for good in 1957, the site becoming Shelton's.

Market Square, 28 June 1929. Prince George accompanied by Major Staton walks towards the Guildhall with the new bank building behind him, inspecting the Guard of Honour lining his route around the city during the Civic Week celebrations.

The extended electricity station, 28 June 1929. Prince George, later Duke of Kent, addresses the crowd before pressing the button to open the extension to the station. Also on the platform are Mrs Blagden, the bishop's wife, Lord Exeter, Frank Hodges of the CEB and the mayor in civic regalia.

28 June 1929. The city was extremely proud of the visit by Prince George and the streets were elaborately decorated with imitation pylons, flags and garlands. A military and 'old soldiers' Guard of Honour lines the route. Peterborough's old soldiers at this time included men who survived both the First World War and the second Boer War, a special force of twenty-six volunteers from the city's Redcoats and Greycoats having been sent to South Africa in 1900. Note the people hanging out of the windows to catch a glimpse of the royal car on its way to the new Town Hall in Bridge Street.

Town Hall, 1929. This foundation stone was placed by Prince George during Civic Week. The construction of the new Town Hall changed the Bridge Street area of the city considerably as the eastern side of Narrow Bridge Street had to be demolished to accommodate it. These men worked for the local building firm of John Thompson, contracted to undertake the work. The company went into voluntary liquidation before the building was completed, but the workmen were kept on.

Peterborough Show, 1907. The Peterborough Show was the forerunner of the present East of England show, held at Alwalton since 1965. An important social and trade occasion, it was organised by the Peterborough Agricultural Society, and people travelled from all over the eastern counties to attend. It began in 1797 in the city, moving to Broadway in 1858 and later to Millfield near Adams Windmill in about 1882. Thirty years later it had settled at Eastfield Road. Between 1921 and 1957 the show was orchestrated by PAS Secretary Mr Robert Bibby, and under his guidance grew to fill the Eastfield showground. A memorial to him was unveiled at Eastfield by Princess Alice, Duchess of Gloucester, on 16 July 1958.

Peterborough Show, 8 July 1909. This picture of Webb's trade stand, with its elaborate façade, reveals the importance of the show to regional businesses. Other firms exhibiting included Singer, the sewing machine manufacturer, Mott's livestock medicines and Barford & Perkins, makers of agricultural machinery.

Peterborough Fête, August 1895. This picture is titled the 'Fated Balloon' and captures the tragic events of one August Bank Holiday. The balloon was part of the act of Mademoiselle Adelaide Bassett, a lady parachutist who toured the country fairs, jumping from the balloon into expectant crowds below. Unfortunately on this occasion the balloon hit a tree and became entangled in telegraph wires. Mademoiselle Bassett must have panicked for at just 200 ft she leapt from the basket to her death.

Church Army wagon, c. 1910. Church missions were very popular with churches of all denominations, being undertaken to raise funds and gather new members. Vans with a message were common sights at rural fairs and in city streets on market days.

Bridge Town, 7 October 1929. The procession to proclaim the opening of Bridge Fair makes its way to the fairground across the town bridge led by the Dean & Chapter's High Bailiff, the Town Beadle, the Town Clerk, W.T. Mellows and the Mayor, Arthur Craig. At the turn of the century concern was expressed that the procession had become outdated and spectators unruly and disrespectful. Judging by the numbers lining the route here interest had revived.

Bridge Fair, c. 1895. This had been a Peterborough occasion since the city was granted its charter by Henry VI in 1439. Traditionally held over three days, 21–3 September, every year, it was originally sited at Fletton Common but in the nineteenth century the date changed to the first week of October. This added to its success as visitors and travelling shows had easier access to the showground. The fair was composed of fairground rides still common today with drinking tents, trade stalls, coconut shies, freak show exhibits and fast food retailers – usually selling shellfish and pickles and pies.

Showboats, Bridge Fair, *c.* 1898. This picture reveals the extent to which Bridge Fair had diverged from its origins as an agricultural festival to one predominantly run to entertain people from all over the Midlands. Travelling players, film shows and brass bands were just a few of the attractions on offer as the fair moved into the twentieth century.

Bridge Fair, 1889. A steam-powered Wurlitzer was just one of the show's attractions. Small steam engines also made it possible to run merry-go-rounds, which were beautifully designed with exotic animals and traditional prancing horses.

Sideshows, Bridge Fair, c. 1895. If this was 'Suetts 77th visit' (below) to Bridge Fair then they had been attending since 1818! Sideshows were an important feature of the fair, selling clothing, sweets and bric-a-brac. These stalls frequently spread along the city streets up into Long Causeway, and agricultural workers often saved their wages from the harvest to buy a winter outfit during the fair.

Mr Hunt's field, Marholm, 28 June 1912. This picture commemorates the landing at Peterborough of the so-called *Daily Mail* airman Mr McEwen – an intrepid pilot who took up a challenge offered by the national paper. He flew his 80 h.p. biplane to Peterborough on his way to Lincoln. The event caused considerable excitement and Peterborough honoured him with a presentation and rose-bowl, given by Councillor Charles Crawley.

Peterborough fields, Walton, 29 June 1912. Following his rapturous welcome at Peterborough, Mr Ewen gave a number of flying exhibitions before leaving for Lincoln. His plane ditched just after taking off, though, causing considerable damage, but fortunately the pilot escaped unhurt. Three days later, following hasty repair work, he was able to continue his journey.

WORK IN FEN & FACTORY

Newborough Duck Decoy, c. 1892. Mr J.B. Williams is seen here encouraging ducks along the elaborately crafted decoy. These were common sights in the Fens, with tame wildfowl being trained to entice other birds into their confines. In the nineteenth century Peterborough market sold large quantities of teal, wild duck, mallard and widgeon to townspeople and to the London meat markets. Carts pulled by two horses, loaded high, left the city twice a week for the capital.

Peterborough Fenlands, *c.* 1910. The three men here are operating a hay press built by local business Barford Perkins. The increase in mechanisation of agricultural practices may have begun but note that the hay still appears to be cut by scythe, as one man carries a blade and all wear leather leg guards.

Men at work gathering a celery harvest, Peterborough fields, 1930s. The beautiful cart carries a plate naming the owner, F.H. Allen, Boro Fen North.

Westgate, before 1900. A Fowler steam ploughing engine makes its way through the city. The traditional methods of agriculture were radically altered by such inventions, rendering many Fen workers redundant as working the land became less labour intensive.

possibly the same Fowler steam ploughing engine, here making its way through Boroughbury, before 1900. To the left are the premises of Mr Thompson, undertaker, and to the right the malt tower and Squire's Brewery, later the headquarters of the Peterborough Liberal Party.

Custom House, *c.* 1910. The old toll-house probably dates from the eighteenth century. At the beginning of the following century river traffic travelling upstream to Northampton or downstream to Wisbech stopped here to pay tolls. Simpson & Mewburn's passenger boats to Wisbech sailed from the quay. With the advent of the railways the quay's use declined and the Custom House was taken over by the Sea Cadets in 1942.

River Nene, from above the old Peterborough Bridge and before the railway viaduct, *c.* 1875. To the right is a new brick house, the home of the Peterborough Rowing Club, founded in the 1870s. The bank is also the site of Woodston and Thomas Hill's wharves, which housed grain and malt for brewing.

Albert Meadow, with the tower of the electricity generating station (opened 22 December 1900) dominating the area now known as Rivergate, *c.* 1910. In 1901 the station met with great resistance from the Gas Company (set up by Mr Sawyer in 1868), as it reduced the city's dependency on gas for light and power, while paving the way for industrial expansion. The station became part of the National Grid in 1948. The pinnacles of the cathedral, the tower of St John's church and the Wentworth Street Methodist chapel are clearly visible in the background.

North bank of the River Nene, *c.* 1895. On the far bank can be seen the boat yard of Mr Alcock and the timber business of J.S. Clarke & Co.

Brink, Wisbech, *c.* 1940: an unfortunate end for one of the Dutch barges (Humber Keel) which used to carry grain along the Nene from Wisbech to the mills at Peterborough. River traffic along this route was a constant source of local argument as silting problems caused grounding of heavy vessels. Peterborough's port development was severely hampered by the lack of dredging to the east.

Lincoln Road, with Adam's Mill, Millfield, on the right, *c.* 1910. The picture provides a neat juxtaposition of new and old industries in Peterborough. Before the advent of electricity, which brought manufacturing and trams to the city, its economy rested almost entirely on local agriculture and market trade – as the street name Cowgate testifies. Just before the six-sailed mill, once owned by the prominent Congregationalist Mr Adams, is J.W. Rowe, builders' merchants. Near here, until 1812, were the city's gallows. The tower of the mill was demolished in 1937 and the site became Adams's garage.

J. Andrews's coal office, Priestgate, *c.* 1905. J. Wood's tricycle, probably purchased from Julyan's or Goodman's cycle shops in the city, stands sentry outside his shed next door. Coal was an important fuel for Peterborough industries, and during the coal strikes at the beginning of the century peat was sold at exorbitant prices from barges near the Customs House.

GNR station coal siding, *c.* 1939: a last trip for the steam road engine owned by Peterborough Gas Company, shown here with a full trailer at the coal siding on the south side of North station. The Gas Company had been set up in 1829, and bought by Mr Sawyer, an ironmonger from Narrow Street, in 1846. He extended gas mains from Fengate to Thorpe and from Walton to Fletton Lane, thus replacing the city's oil-fired street-lamps with gas lights.

Warboy's Brickyard, *c.* 1910. These men dug clay from pits at Fletton which was made into bricks by hand. Fletton 'plastic clay' was a distinctive grey colour and dried very well owing to its bed of Oxford shale. Many small local brickworks existed during the nineteenth century. Most amalgamated in the 1920s to form the London Brick Company.

Peterborough fish market, 1939. This was held at the Spital Locomotive Depot by the track-side. The railway made trading with London markets such as Billingsgate much easier.

Central Sugar Factory, Peterborough, 1940. The sugar-beet factory was established in 1926 during the Depression, bringing much-needed employment. It considerably enhanced local beet farming, helping to raise productivity. During the Second World War the company relied heavily on women workers to take part in the government's sugar-beet campaign.

The plate shop, Baker-Perkins, 7 March 1922. This famous local firm, formed by the amalgamation of Werner Pfleiderer and Perkins, a London engineering firm, was attracted to Peterborough in 1904 by the rail network, open land and cheap labour. During the First World War the company changed its name to Perkins Engineers despite the fact that recruits from the plant were known locally as 'Werners Own'. In 1920 the Baker family bought into the firm and in 1923 it became Baker-Perkins Ltd.

Union march, Cromwell Road, c. 1910. Peterborough's Trades Union movement began in earnest with the railway workers, their strikes of 1919 bringing the city's industries almost to a standstill. The city is proud of its historical association with NALGO, the now national union that was founded at the Bedford Coffee House on 14 November 1896.

PUBLIC SERVICE & NATURAL DISASTER

Louis Stanley Jast, Peterborough's first public librarian, c. 1897. Appointed in 1892 as Chief Librarian at the City Library in Park Road, he was one of the first to implement the newly devised Dewey Decimal system, now commonplace in libraries all over the world. A distinctive figure about town, he encouraged local societies to pool resources to build up the public library. He left Peterborough in 1898 and his career culminated with his appointment to the presidency of the National Library Association. He died in 1944 in Twickenham.

The new public library, Broadway, 29 May 1906. The official opening ceremony was attended by Mr Andrew Carnegie, who offered the £6,000 required to build it in 1903. Also on the platform is Mr J.H. Beeby, Chairman of the Library Committee. The previous city library was established in the Fitzwilliam Hall in Park Road by Dr Thomas Walker in 1892. With the demands of an increasingly literate population, larger premises were required and this purpose-built library came into use from 2 December 1905. After the opening ceremony, Mr Carnegie was awarded the Freedom of the City at the Guildhall.

J.W. Bodger's shop, Cowgate, c. 1910. Mr Bodger's contribution to Peterborough is of continuing significance. Born in Broad Bridge Street in 1856 above his father's grocery shop, he left school at fourteen and became apprenticed to Sturton & Sons in the same street. After qualifying as a pharmacist he set up this shop where he worked until his retirement in 1914. He worked tirelessly for the city. He helped with excavation of the Roman villa at Castor and was a member of the local branch of the League of Nations Union. In 1873 Mr Bodger became Honorary Secretary of the Peterborough Natural History, Scientific and Archaeological Society (later the Museum Society). An avid local historian, he kept the society's burgeoning exhibits in his home until a museum was founded in Park Road. He was awarded a Fellowship of the Linnaean Society in 1920 and died on 12 February 1939. His private collection is now housed at the City Museum in Priestgate.

J.W. Bodger (Museum Secretary), Dame Madge Kendal and Mr J.T.S. Flynn (editor of the *Peterborough Citizen*) pictured outside the museum in Priestgate on 30 May 1932. The occasion marked is the presentation by Dame Madge of her grandfather's eighteenth-century make-up box to the City. A highly regarded actress, her connection with Peterborough arises through her grandfather, J.W. Robertson, who was lessee of the Peterborough Theatre at the turn of the nineteenth century. Dame Madge followed family tradition and became a frequent visitor to the City in travelling performances.

Peterborough Museum, Park Road, at the rear of the Theatre Royal, pictured between 1923 and 1929 when it occupied this site. The sign on the right gives the name of J.W. Bodger, then the museum's curator. He was aided in the establishment of the city museum by James Harrison 'Postcard' Smith, Honorary Botanical Curator. His botanical exhibitions were locally famous.

The City Infirmary, Priestgate, *c.* 1910, before it became the Peterborough City Museum & Art Gallery. Built in 1816 by Squire Cooke, the imposing Georgian façade of his home reflects the fashion for Greek Classical style at the time. It was sold to Earl Fitzwilliam in 1856, and he exchanged it with the Dispensary building in Milton Street. Thus it became the City's Infirmary until 1928 when the War Memorial Hospital in Midland Road was opened. Built with three storeys, the two-storey wings are later additions paid for by public subscription on the occasions of Queen Victoria's jubilee in 1897 and the coronation of King Edward VII in 1902. The Museum Society took over the premises on 22 June 1931.

War Memorial Hospital, Midland Road, *c.* 1930. This hospital, built at the suggestion of Mayor George Nicholls, replaced the Infirmary in Priestgate and had 154 beds. The foundation stone was laid in 1925, and it became a lasting tribute to the men of Peterborough who died in the First World War. Officially opened in June 1928 by Field Marshal Sir William Robertson, it was completed in 1929 with the opening of a children's wing by Prince George during the Civic Week celebrations.

Peterborough police force, 1929. The city's first 'peelers' began operating in the city in 1836 but a more effective force was created by the newly formed City Council in 1874. The unit comprised a head constable, two sergeants and twelve constables, and was based in Milton Street. It remained here until 1949 when some of the police moved to Westwood Airfield and the others moved to the Guildhall. The street decorations show that the city was celebrating Prince George's visit.

Two peterborough firemen, 1941.

Sessions House, Thorpe Road, *c.* 1900. The rather eccentric façade of the Sessions House was built for the Liberty Magistrates in 1842, fashioned by the Victorian architect W.J. Donthorne in the style of a Norman castle. Prisoners were actually housed in now demolished buildings behind this main entrance. By 1878 the gaol was redundant, changes in administration and an increasing prison population requiring detainees to be despatched to Cambridge or Northampton. It became the headquarters of the 'Liberty of Peterborough' Police Force and a magistrates' court.

Law Courts, New Road, before 1899. A monument to Victorian design, the distinctive brick County Court was built in 1873 to house the Circuit Judge and Registrar of the County Court. Law-keeping in Peterborough was originally the responsibility of the Lord Paramount who had his own jail and the Dean and Chapter whose prison was in the cathedral precincts. There were three courts in the city: the Manor Court held twice yearly, the Court of Common Pleas held once a week and the Court of Pie Powder (pieds poudreux), which took place on market days to deal with trading disputes.

Town Hall, shortly after it was opened. The Town Hall was completed in 1933 to replace the fragmentary accommodation of council offices about the city. The design was chosen by open competition, with the winner, E. Berry Webber, proposing this dignified Corinthian portico, behind which is the Mayor's Parlour. The interior is striking, particularly the staircase and the classic 1930s fittings.

Trade Exhibition at the Town Hall, c. 1950. The firm of Robert Sayle occupied the store belonging to Cornelius Thompson in King Street. It had the city's first electrically powered lifts and a distinctive bridge over the street connecting its two halves. It was destroyed by fire in 1956. Apart from the stands the hall itself is worthy of note. The elegant lamps and mirrors reveal the pride in its construction.

Peterborough City Fire Brigade, 9 August 1886. Men of the Peterborough Fire Brigade are on a visit to the works of Messrs Merryweather & Sons, makers of fire engines. They actually purchased the machine around which they are standing. It was the city's first steam appliance and made a considerable difference to the effectiveness of their fire-fighting.

An atmospheric shot of the City Fire Brigade operating hoses on a real or imaginary fire, Market Square, *c.* 1897. Note the crowds massing at the junction of Long Causeway. The photographer secured an excellent vantage point from somewhere near the Midland Bank site.

Brainsby's fire, Cumbergate, January 1898. The total ruin of Brainsby's carriage works occurred just the day before the firm received one of its biggest orders.

This picture was taken to commemorate the winning of the National Hose Cart competition at Crystal Palace in 1912. The six recruits are shown in Brook's Yard. The volunteer service was housed in the coach house of the Angel Hotel before moving to Church Street and then King Street in 1922. Members included Alderman Whitsted, Secretary of Peterborough Football and Cricket Clubs, and Alex Snowden, Captain of the City Rugby Club (1950–5).

Peterborough Volunteer Fire Brigade, 1900. Seventeen of Peterborough's fire fighters photographed outside the fire station after they had won the brigade championship at Crystal Palace. The man standing to the right of the ladder is Chief Fire Officer, Honorary Captain John C. Gill, also the city's first electrical engineer.

Westwood Works, 23 March 1922. The 'great fire' at the Westwood Works of Baker Perkins devastated one of Peterborough's most important engineering businesses. The damage was estimated at over £25,000 and the factory had to be completely rebuilt. When the blaze was exacerbated by the explosion of oxygen cylinders, additional fire services had to be brought in from Old Fletton and the Midland Railway to help extinguish it.

Queen Street Baptist church fire, 16 October 1905. This picture clearly shows the effect of an unexplained fire that swept through the church. The Barrass Memorial Hall next door was also seriously damaged. Services continued on the following Sunday at the Theatre Royal. The Baptists moved soon after to a new church in Park Road. Notice the Brigade fire escape. This was housed near the Butter Cross and was bought by the City Corporation in 1889.

Lincoln Road, 28 March 1916. The Great Storm of 1916 was one of the worst storms ever recorded in the region. It brought down over sixty telegraph poles between Peterborough and Deeping. People were trapped in their homes, and tram and railway services completely halted.

Midgate, 1912. Freak weather was evidently no stranger to the city. This picture shows the havoc caused by floods. Another cloudburst in June 1924 left this area of the city almost impassable. The shops in Midgate at that time included one of T.L. Barrett's stores, which took over the house on the immediate right, the Lewis cycle factory and the offices of the City Finance Department. Probably very few were open for business!

Stanground, 1916. In the last week of August the rainfall was the highest ever recorded in the city and Stanground was covered in up to 4 ft of water. Crops were totally ruined and people were trapped upstairs in their homes. Being Fen dwellers the people of Peterborough had evidently learnt to be resourceful.

Fen Drain, Peterborough, 1939. The men here are busy filling bags with earth in order to reinforce the banks of one of the fen drains. 1939 proved to be another year of heavy rainfall and floods in the area.

CITY TRANSPORT

Corn Exchange, c. 1880. The wagonette parked here at the side of the Corn Exchange could carry eight passengers and evidently a great deal of luggage, possibly bought in the adjacent Market Square. This form of transport became less common after the introduction of horse-drawn omnibus services around the city. The Corn Exchange, built in 1846, replaced the small Queen Street Theatre built in 1774 on Butchers Row. It had capacity for a thousand people and was at one time the busiest in England. The Corn Exchange was badly damaged by an incendiary bomb during the Second World War and was demolished in 1964.

The horse and trap of the Peterborough Equitable and Industrial Co-operative Society may be parked near one of the city's two railway stations, prime locations for carriage drivers and advertisers, *c.* 1900. The large poster depicting the attractions of Blackpool may be the work of the Thomas Cook company. Since the nineteenth century Thomas Cook had organised holidays and rail journeys to prominent social occasions, including the Crystal Palace exhibitions.

Session House, Thorpe Road, *c.* 1893. Crowson's carrier's cart is piled high with chairs, and advertises removal services all around the Peterborough region. Carts of this kind were common at the turn of the century, travelling into the city for markets on Wednesday and Saturday from outlying villages. They averaged just 2 m.p.h. owing to the number of stops they made.

Cromwell Road, *c.* 1896. This busy street scene was possibly photographed on market day or before an election result. The horse-drawn double-decker buses shown here could carry up to thirty passengers and were operating in Peterborough from about 1875.

Long Causeway, *c.* 1905. An uneasy relationship is shown here at the junction of Market Place and Long Causeway. The omnibus may be one of the fleet owned by Mr William Bailey whose business began in 1896. For a time the horse-drawn double-decker bus operators such as Charles Baldwin and John Casbon competed with the electric trams which appeared in January 1903. The demise of the trams in 1930 was preceded by an unsuccessful attempt to run a motor bus service in 1904, and regular services by the outbreak of the First World War.

A busy day in Long Causeway with both trams full of shoppers, *c.* 1905. Tram routes from Peterborough city centre ran out to the villages of Dogsthorpe and Newark, to Millfield and Walton. Their installation required over 30 miles of overhead cabling.

Long Causeway, *c.* 1920. Tram number 12 enters Market Square carrying an advertisement for Messrs Claypole and Sons' piano and organ shop. Their premises in Narrow Bridge Street were the booking office for the Theatre Royal. In 1903 twelve trams were put into operation. They were double-deckers, open to the sky on top and the fare was 2*d.* The success of this enterprise led to the addition of two more trams in 1906.

Long Causeway, decorated for a visit by the Prince of Wales, July 1923. On the left is the shop of Paten & Co., wine sellers, and further up at 18 Long Causeway is one of Neaverson's famous tea-shops. The Neaverson empire extended to shops in Broad Bridge Street and Bridge End.

Broad Bridge Street, c. 1920. Note the absence of tramlines in Broad Bridge Street and the more traditional horse-drawn cart alongside the motor-car.

Long Causeway, *c.* 1905. Goodman and Son's cycle shop was run from premises behind Cash & Co., where they also gave cycling lessons. It sold bicycles and tricycles made by manufacturers whose names are still familiar today, including Raleigh, Triumph and Singer.

T. Goodman & Co. with their own shop-front, Long Causeway, *c.* 1888. The Goodmans had been traders in Peterborough since Feast Goodman set up his grocer's shop in Westgate in 1800. The change to selling cycles was a shrewd one. The flat local terrain and the dry climate, together with the city's main factories being situated on the outskirts, made it ideal for cycling both for work and pleasure.

Peterborough Tricycle Club, 1888 or 1889. The city has a long cycling history. In 1875 the Amateur Cycling Club joined the Tricycle Club to form the Peterborough Cycling Club, thought to be the oldest in the world. Other cycling clubs emerged, including a ladies' group, which merged with the men's club in 1898 for reasons of safety. Rallies were held all over the region, the sport having become very fashionable. In 1904 local cycling hero 'Dubs' Robertson competed at the third Olympics in St Louis, USA. This photograph was taken to celebrate the introduction of the pneumatic tyre.

Great Northern Railway station, *c.* 1910: an unusually quiet view of the main approach to this exceptionally busy station. The array of advertising testifies to the durability of consumer tastes. The Stone's office was situated in Midgate, opposite Long Causeway; their factory was in Monument Street and Crawthorne Street

GNR Station, February 1909. The children waiting here patiently in the rain were hoping to see Mr Jack Binns. He was born in Peterborough and in January 1909 became the first person to use the Marconi SOS system to save lives. On this occasion, a month later, his native town honoured him with the presentation of a scroll by the mayor. His medals and gold watch were given to the museum in 1961.

GNR station looking south, *c.* 1895. The goods office to the right was demolished in January 1978. The hoarding in the centre carries an advertisement for Barrett's shop, known locally as Waterloo House, which dominated one corner of Long Causeway. The donkey cart recalls the story of Peterborough's famous donkey, Jimmy. A German pack animal born during the Battle of the Somme, he was found orphaned by the 1st Scottish Rifles and adopted as their mascot. Demobilised in 1919, Jimmy was bought by Mrs Heath of Lincoln Road, Peterborough, to help raise funds for the local RSPCA. He died in his paddock in Burghley Square (now Clifton House) on 10 May 1943.

Interior of GNR station, *c.* 1895. In the nineteenth century Peterborough had three railway stations. The GNR is now known simply as Peterborough station as the East station was demolished in 1972 and the Midland station only operated between 1858 and 1866. At the time of this photograph the GNR station had eight trains a day to King's Cross. Note the separate waiting rooms for men and women. The roof proved typical of Victorian engineering, withstanding a bomb explosion in 1942.

GER station staff, *c.* 1905. This assembly of front-line railwaymen includes porters, ticket inspectors, guards and the station-master in GER uniform.

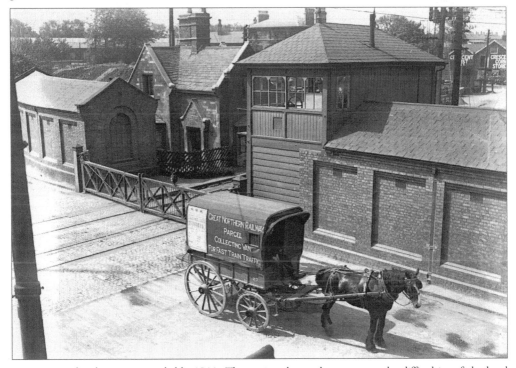

GNR station level-crossing, probably 1911. This patient horse demonstrates the difficulties of the level crossing near the Northern station. Here the lines of the GNR and Midland Railway ran in parallel. Carts and pedestrians could be caught between them for some time as trains entered the station.

GNR station subway, Thorpe Road, *c.* 1905. In 1881 Mrs Marion Dunn was killed at the double-gated level crossing where the GNR lines ran alongside those of the Midland Railway. This subway was built under the lines to satisfy public demands for a safer crossing while proposals for a bridge were being debated.

GNR station subway, River Lane, *c.* 1913: the same scene after Crescent Bridge (arching on the left), named after the row of houses demolished in its wake, opened in 1913. Both the subway and level crossing were then closed and Thorpe Road renamed River Lane. Almost all of the buildings seen here have since been demolished.

Level crossing, Thorpe Road, 1913. Peterborians have always enjoyed civic occasions and hundreds of people attended the last procession over the GNR level crossing before the opening of Crescent Bridge, led by the Mayoress J.G. Barford, Chief Constable Danby, the Beadle carrying the mace, the Town Clerk and other civic dignitaries together with a police escort and officials from the GNR, including Sir Frederick Fison, Director of the GNR (1884–1922). Note the boarded-up subway on the right.

Crescent Bridge, 1913. The new Crescent Bridge was opened to the public on 16 April 1913 amidst great ceremony and at the considerable cost of nearly £34,000. Afterwards a formal dinner was held at the Great Northern Railway Hotel for the Mayoress J.G. Barford, the Town Clerk, and GNR and Corporation officials.

Peterborough Crescent Junction signal box,1950s. Sited to the south of Peterborough North station, this box controlled movements to and from the GNR tracks in the foreground. The box closed in March 1973.

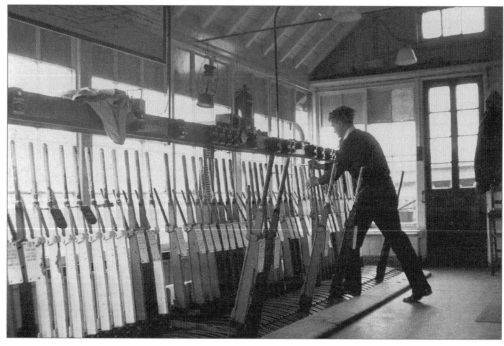

Eastfield signal box, *c.* 1920. The line through Peterborough to London was designed by Joseph Locke for Edmund Denison, and built by Thomas Brassey who entered Peterborough aboard the very first train from London on 7 August 1851. The original Eastfield signal box is still in use in today, controlling the yards and goods lines in the Westwood Bridge area.

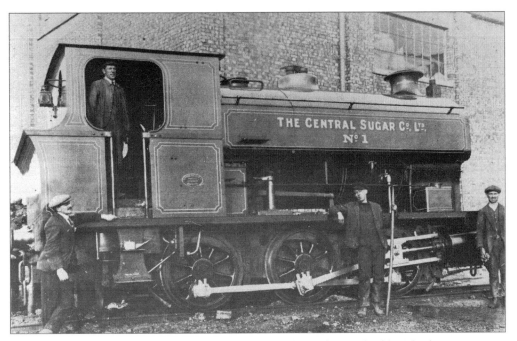

The advent of the railways changed the industry of Peterborough considerably. This locomotive, no. 1945, was built for the Central Sugar Company in 1926. Their choice of the city for a new factory at least partially alleviated Peterborough's high level of unemployment during the years of the Depression.

GNR Depot, c. 1915. GNR 2–6–0 no. 1654 was photographed with thirty-three women engine cleaners during the First World War.

GNR locomotive no. 1001 in New England yard, March 1895. Sir Henry Royce of Rolls-Royce was a locomotive apprentice at New England in 1901. His early promise was fulfilled with the construction of his first two-cylinder 10 h.p. car in 1904.

Station sidings, 4 January 1865. Steam engine accidents were not uncommon and this picture shows the carnage wrought by a boiler explosion on a Saturday evening in Peterborough. The wreckage damaged nearby engine sheds: note the funnel at the bottom left. On 14 August 1922 a train overran the buffers and partly demolished a house close to Crescent Bridge.

An engaging picture of track layers or wagon repairers from the GER depot, *c.* 1905.

GNR School, New England, 1890s. The GNR established locomotive works at New England in 1853. Within the next ten years the community of railway workers and their families had grown into a small town, known locally (and uncharitably) as 'The Barracks'. New England had its own pubs and shops, chapel, parish church, and even a permanent local school built by the GNR.

Great Northern Hotel, 2 March 1892. This photo was taken from the excellent vantage-point afforded by the nearby station roof. The Great Northern Hotel was owned by the GNR and had a fleet of horse-drawn carriages to ferry its visitors to and from the city centre. The first licensee when it opened in 1852 was Thomas Percival.

GNR locomotive 2–2–2 no. 880 and a local passenger train at Peterborough North station, between 1894 and 1903. Despite the noise and smoke, the steam engine retains a glamour that modern train travel cannot supply.

New Road near the junction of Crawthorne Road, *c.* 1938. Clarke Brothers' car showroom is displaying six Hillman cars. One of the city's first garages was Murkett's which was run from the former Golden Lion Commercial Hotel in Bridge Street. As car ownership increased in Peterborough the pressure on city streets became acute. At one time the Market Square was graced with a complicated box junction and the west front of the cathedral had to be cleaned because of air pollution in 1972.

WARTIME

A salutary reminder of the realities of war: St Peter's College Memorial, c. 1918. St Peter's Training College was established in 1864 and built to an elegant design by Sir George Gilbert Scott. It was founded for the education and training of schoolmasters for the region.

Army Recruiting Office, the west side of Long Causeway, September 1914. Hundreds of Peterborough men flocked to enlist after the outbreak of the First World War was announced in the city in August 1914. Mayor Winfrey's recruiting speech in October increased the number joining up, leaving local industry with a serious shortfall in their workforce. The optimism with which the men enlisted was to be brutally short.

Werners Own, September 1914: the eager faces of a host of new recruits assembling near the GNR station. They became known locally as 'Werners Own' because they all came from the engineering factory later owned by Baker Perkins and called Werner Pfleiderer and Perkins until anti-German feeling rendered it necessary to rename the company.

GNR station, September 1914. New recruits are met at the station by a brass band. Peterborough men were willing volunteers. Alderman Isaac Whitsted formed his own battalion in 1914, known as 'Whitsted's Own'; they were later merged with the 7th Northants Regiment.

Troops on parade, Cromwell Road, near the junction with Westgate, 1914. 'A city of khaki' was how Peterborough was described during the First World War. Many regiments were quartered in the city, including the 5th Essex Battalion, the Norfolk and Suffolk Army Service Corps 4th & 5th Battalions and the Norfolk Regiment. These troops were billeted on townspeople around the streets at Gladstone Road, Russell Street, Bright Street and Lincoln Road. Their presence was a boon to local trade and, given the number of sons absent from their homes, fighting in France or manning coastal defences, they were well looked after.

Narrow Bridge Street, August 1914. F. Metz, pork butcher, was driven from his home during the riot which followed the announcement of war in 1914. The rioters ransacked his shop, spoiling the meat and breaking windows before moving on to the Salmon & Compasses in Long Causeway. Mayor Winfrey was forced, for the first time, to read the Riot Act in Peterborough and a curfew was imposed on the city's streets.

Long Causeway, c. 1913. The Salmon & Compasses was one of Peterborough's many ale-houses. In August 1914 it was attacked by an angry mob intent on harming the German licensee, Mr Guest. When the riot began to escalate Mayor Winfrey called in the Fire Brigade, who declined to attend as they feared for their equipment. The Yeomanry were eventually able to impose order.

Oundle, 1914. Major Tom Walker leads the Northamptonshire Battery through Oundle on its way to Peterborough, followed by Tptr A.T. Lambert. Note Kitchener's familiar moustached face on the recruiting poster on the Market House and the sign pointing the way 'To the Recruiting Office'.

Newark Hill, Peterborough, 1914. Major Walker reaches the city. Behind Tptr Lambert is Sergeant-Major Simpson.

Narrow Street, *c.* 1914: a parade by the Peterborough Battery, formed in 1908. The officers are Major T.H. Walker, Sergeant-Major Hankins and Staff Sergeant Training Instructor Lambert. In 1915 the Battery, under the command of Major Walker, was sent to France and then Egypt before fighting in Palestine in 1918.

Peterborough Battery Troops, 1939–41. In 1939 the Battery joined the Cambridgeshire regiments in Singapore, where they were captured by enemy forces and served out the war as prisoners of war. The building in the background is the National Silk Workers Union.

Soldiers & Sailors' Rest Home, near the GNR station, *c.* 1917. Peterborough did much to support its war veterans. There were local branches of the Federation of Discharged and Demobilised Soldiers and Sailors, the Soldiers Sailors and Airmen's Families Association and the British Legion. This home was used between 1915 and 1919 for casualties of the First World War and soldiers stopping at Peterborough while waiting for train connections to other parts of the country.

Guildhall, 15 August 1914. These women bearing trays of white roses paraded the city to raise funds for the war effort. Note the sign for the Board of Trade Labour Exchange on the right of the picture. Peterborough's unemployed burgeoned in the 1920s and the Exchange moved to New Road and then to larger premises in Westgate in 1934.

Brick Company, *c.* 1915. In the latter half of the nineteenth century the demand for housing was increasing as the city's population grew. At Peterborough the brick-works at Fletton, established in 1877, used local 'Oxford clay' to make bricks by hand. The back of the photo suggests that these women workers, assisting the war effort, may be E. Shaw and T. Burton.

Engineers' shop, *c.* 1916. The woman in this photograph is named as Miss L. Uff; she is engaged in the production of shell-cases during the First World War at a factory in Peterborough. The women's war effort was in full force in the city with Symington's corset factory engaged in making parachutes.

Engineers' shop, *c.* 1916. This production line shows women greasing and packing shell-cases. The local emphasis on agricultural engineering and precision tool making (as at Baker Perkins and the Newall Engineering Co. at Fletton), made Peterborough a focus for war armament manufacture, particularly given its proximity to rail and water transport.

Anzac's funeral, August 1916. The sad tale of the Anzac who died in Peterborough on 31 July 1916 reveals much about the compassion of the people of the city. Sergeant G.T. Hunter was travelling through Peterborough aboard a Red Cross train heading for Halifax, carrying soldiers wounded during the Battle of the Somme. His spinal injuries were so severe that he was taken from the train to the Infirmary at Priestgate where he died the next day. Public sympathy was roused by the discovery that he was an orphan and the *Peterborough Advertiser* promptly set up a fund to erect a memorial to him. He is remembered with a brass plaque in the cathedral and a Celtic cross above his grave in Old Broadway cemetery. Hundreds of townspeople attended his funeral. Leading this procession is A. Caleb Taylor, Hospital Secretary, who in 1897 made and operated the region's first Röntgen X-ray machine at the Infirmary. He died of the ill-effects in 1927.

Outside the Magistrate's clerk's office, Church Street, 1940. Members of the Women's Voluntary Service are collecting aluminium utensils as part of the nationwide drive to manufacture aeroplanes. The pans appear remarkably shiny!

Church Street, c. 1940. The WVS mobile canteen outside the police station with St John's church in the background. The WVS was run by Mrs A.H. Mellows, who admirably co-ordinated the efforts of 3,000 women to cope with the influx of troops to the city, from Poland, Eastern Europe and America during the Second World War.

Thorpe Road Hospital, 1939. The ARP is shown here engaged in sandbagging the operating theatre at the hospital at the commencement of the Second World War. The ARP manned sixty-five air-raid shelters in the city during the war.

No. 67 London Road, 16 November 1940. Mr and Mrs Hardy and their daughter occupied this house and were asleep when it suffered a direct hit by a German bomb. Miraculously they survived unhurt. Peterborough was subjected to bombardment during the Second World War, the worst period being 1942 when more than 200 incendiaries fell on city streets.

Bridge Street, June 1940. A German bombing raid over East Anglia caused some roof and window damage to rooms above Gibson's Café, later the Elephant & Castle public house. Business seems to have been unaffected.

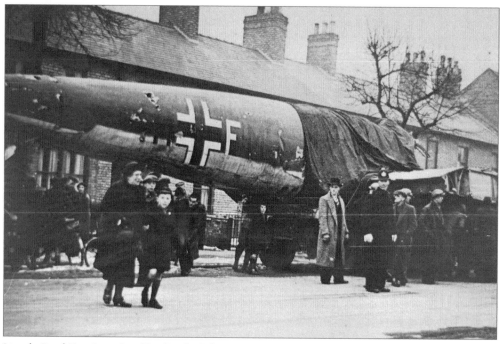

Lincoln Road East (now Burghley Road), February 1940. A truly striking sight: the unidentified fuselage of a crashed German bomber passing through Peterborough on the back of a lorry; it had been shot down in the north of England. Air attacks on the city were mitigated by the efforts of the coastal defences.

King's School, *c.* 1942. A crashed German Junker Ju88 bomber on view to the public at the King's School sports field, with Huntly Grove in the background, drew large crowds of schoolboys, here in the foreground, and townspeople.

An exuberant display of tea, 'now off ration', possibly in the window of the Co-operative Society in Park Road, *c.* 1950. The ticket in the top right-hand corner reads 'Peterborough Chamber of Trade, Window Display Competition, Class 1, Things To Eat'. It was awarded second place.

St Paul's Church grounds, with a glimpse of Lincoln Road in the background, 1947. Children play their instruments under the direction of an enthusiastic conductor!

ACKNOWLEDGEMENTS

The author wishes to thank all the staff of the Peterborough City Museum & Art Gallery for their help during the making of this book and for their interest & encouragement, particularly Elizabeth St Hill Davies & Dr Gordon Chancellor who gave permission to use photographs from the museum archives, and Mr John Strangward for aiding the compilation procedure considerably.

Thanks are also due to Mr Richard Hillier of Peterborough Central (Local Studies) Library whose initial advice and last-minute co-operation proved invaluable and for giving permission to use pictures from the library collection in this work. The Local Studies Library is recommended to anyone with an interest in the history of Peterborough. I must also thank Simon Fletcher at Sutton Publishing for his guidance during this project.

Lastly, my grateful thanks go to Stuart Roberts and to my family for their practical help and ever present support. This book is dedicated to them.

BIBLIOGRAPHY

Austin, G.D., *Peterborough Trams* (Public Library, 1975)

Bendixson, Terence, *The Peterborough Effect, Reshaping a City* (Peterborough Development Corporation, 1988)

Bevis, Trevor, *Snippets From Old Peterborough* (Trevor Bevis, 1994)

Bracey, Denis, *The Book of Peterborough* (Barracuda Books, 1985)

Bull, J. and V., *Peterborough, A Portrait In Old Picture Postcards — Volume 1* (SB Publications, 1988)

Bull, J. and V. and McKenzie, R., *Peterborough Then & Now, A Portrait In Photographs & Old Postcards* (SB Publications, 1992)

Bull, J. and V., Perry, S. and Sturgess, R., *Peterborough, A Portrait In Old Picture Postcards — Volume 3* (SB Publications, 1990)

Hillier, Richard, *Old Peterborough In Photographs,* (ed. Allan Bunch, Cambridgeshire Libraries & City of Peterborough Museum & Art Gallery, 1979)

Cartwright, J.L., *Peterborough Cathedral* (Jarrold & Sons Ltd, 1967)

Dack, C., *Old Peterborough Customs* (1899)

Dane, R.A., *Railways of Peterborough* (Greater Peterborough Arts Council, 1978)

Liquorice, Mary (ed.), *Posh Folk* (Cambridgeshire Libraries Publications, 1991)

Mackreth, Donald, *Peterborough* (Alan Sutton Publishing, 1994)

Perry, S., *Peterborough, A Portrait In Old Picture Postcards — Volume 2* (SB Publications, 1989)

Tebbs, H.F., *How The City Has Changed* (Sharman & Co. Ltd, Peterborough, 1975)

Tebbs, H.F., *Peterborough* (The Oleander Press, Cambridge, 1979)

Webb, Leslie, *Some Peterborough Buildings* (The Peterborough Society, 1986)